W9-AXG-226

Anne Geddes

Welcome to the world of Anne Geddes.

The images used in this counting book are taken from Anne's latest collective work entitled *Down in the Garden.*

Anne has remarked that "Children are the true believers, and some of us are lucky enough to make the transition to adulthood without losing the ability to see through young eyes."

We know that you will enjoy sharing time with your children as you experience with them the unique and enchanting images contained in the *Down in the Garden Counting Book.*

ANNE GEDDES™

ISBN 1-55912-345-1

Published in 1996 by
Cedco Publishing Company
2955 Kerner Boulevard
San Rafael, CA 94901

Second Printing, January 1997
Designed by Denise Elliott
Produced by Kel Geddes
Typeset by Image Design
Images first published in *Down in the Garden*
Color Separations by Image Centre
Printed by South China Printing Co. Ltd, Hong Kong

ANNE GEDDES

Down in the Garden

COUNTING BOOK

Cedco

1

One butterfly

2
Two mice

3
Three squirrels

4

Four caterpillars

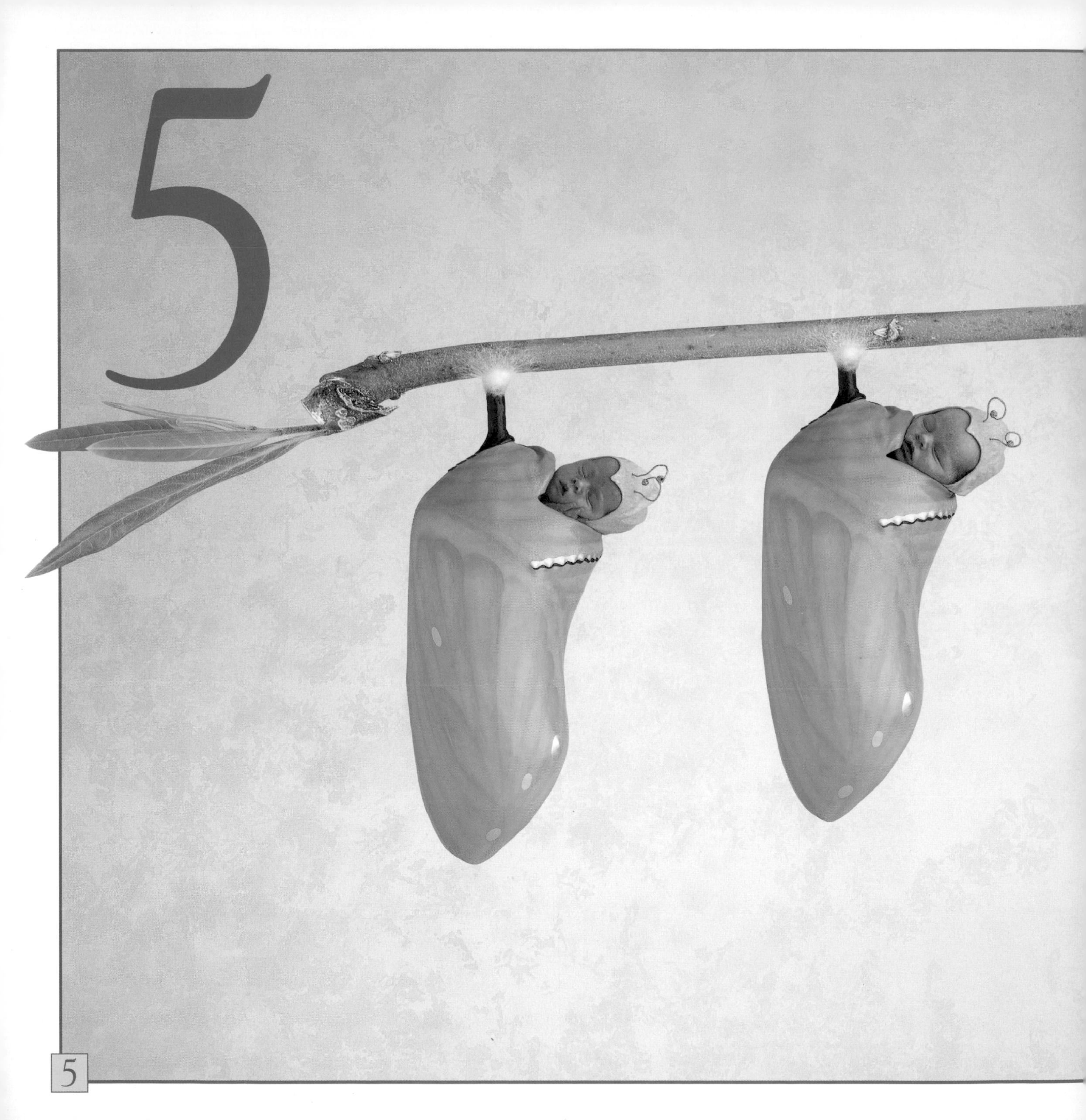
5

Five cocoons

6

Six teddy bears

7

Seven mushrooms

8

Eight fairies

Nine gnomes

10

Ten flowerpots

?

How ma

hedgehogs can you count?

How many birds can you see inside?